"Deor

dear heart dear one"

with
"Core rite"

This is the first edition, 1st August 2007.
Published by justWords limited,
30A St James Place, Mangotsfield, Bristol BS17 3JB UK
Registered in England 2984663.
http://www.justwords.demon.co.uk
orderline: **athais@justwords.demon.co.uk**

ISBN 1-901382-04-4
Copyright © justWords Limited

Designed, produced & managed by AThaiS Limited

Bureau services and advice: Skriptorium Ltd,
6 Lower Park Row, Clifton, Bristol BS1 5BJ UK

justWords is a new diasporas micropublisher

Cover illustration by Siriluck Kedseemake
ภาพหน้าปกวาดโดย สิริลักษณ์ เกตุศรีเมฆ [1]
From an idea by Thomas Albert Fox

is certified a gm[2] free publication.

---

[1] Translation of line above into Thai

[2] gm free: "government money" and "god's money" free. That is free of the hand of committees, councils and the concomitant general crud of special initiatives, lottery funds and other funny money, including corporate sponsors, and especially state or religious cultivation. Independently certified GM free by B F Garret & Co.

Thomas Albert Fox is the author of:

"A Suspicion of Sun"	justWords Ltd	1996
"The Fairy Queen"	justWords Ltd	2002
"Upon Godolphin House & Pengersick Castle"	justWords Ltd	2005
"Epithalamion: Upon the Wedding of George Mihov and Malvina Kotorova Upon this the Sixteenth Day of September 2006CE"	justWords Ltd	2006

Thomas Albert Fox

"D e o r

dear heart dear one"

with
"Core rite"

Edited by Terry Edwards
justWords
http://www.justwords.demon.co.uk

Contents

Acknowledgements and Introduction

The two small poems given here are both about the 'heart'. The first, while presented in a simple and familiar form, expresses a complex interplay between the being of the poet and the being of the deer he named Deor. It is written in a straightforward, simple, if formal manner, that initially shields the reader &/or the auditor ('readitor') from the reactive disenchantment of a sudden surprise meeting with complexity. The intention is to avoid creating immediate discouragement in the hope that the 'readitor' will be drawn into fuller engagement. It is an highly worked piece as the draftings show. The second poem is also simple and direct, but presented in an highly informal, indeed childish manner. Yet, it too is complex, but the drafting shows that it was written in an immediate and highly intuitive manner. Reflection and consideration of the draftings show that both 'heart' poems are equally complex although very differently expressed. Fox, records, captures, perhaps creates, intense emotion by revealing complexity of being through the medium of the English language. Both poems of 'the heart' are expressions of intense emotion. At the core of "Deor *dear heart dear one*" is its layered puns and ambiguities, while at the heart of "Cor rite" (or "Gi' us yr core mate") is its direct transaction with childhood, hunger, friendship, need, and a rite of passage with a tiny Eve. The language of "Core rite" is English as spoken in the 'soufamptun' (Southampton) dialect. Thus the two poems span the English language from Old English through received mid-atlantic to, as it were, the modern Old English of Hampshire, (old) England ('ampshur' - 'wheeze ar 'ampshur 'ogs').

It is unusual for Fox to keep his draftings. He is by nature secretive and in any case usually drafts on the back of loose sheets of scrap paper and then writes up directly to his wordprocessor, shredding and deleting all but the final draft. Not that he treats any work as actually finally finished. By a final draft he means the last effort on that particular piece. Very occasionally he uses old fashioned pen, pencil and notebook. This is when he is far away from home and

1

without a computer. He therefore keeps all the draftings in a notebook until returning to his wordprocessing facilities. Normally, after transferring the then 'final' draft to his computer he destroys all the notebook draftings as scrap paper and also deletes all versions on the computer, except the last. Very occasionally he forgets to cover his tracks, and this is one such occasion which has let me see in its natural state how two of his poems have come about[3].

"Deor *dear heart dear one*" was composed at Connachat Cottage in the heart of Queen Elizabeth II's Balmoral Estate, Scotland, during December 2005. It expresses the direct observation, not of the many deer freely roaming the wilds of the 50,000 acre estate, but of one in particular. It is an expression of the being of the particular deer seen by Fox, and which Siriluck captured momentarily in her camera, and from which she was able to create the intense detail of her beautiful painting for the cover illustration. During their stay at the cottage deer did in fact slip down from the surrounding woods at dusk to graze the lovely green grass growing in a broad strip to its front and south side. They waited timidly until the light had fallen and shadows were formed all around to cover their descent.

Fox found direct affinity with Deor through a momentary exchange of glances. Upon that instant they became one. Not that the deer had become human, but that Fox had become a deer. In this he felt he had overcome that hubristic self-deception by which humankind instinctively obliges 'heris' fellow creatures to succumb to the comforts of that common anthropomorphic delusion, that the human somehow invades the animal by superior intuition. Fox did not feel Deor in this way, but in the shamanistic sense of him becoming Deor, and thus knowing more of the world through that becoming. Paradoxically his humanity was extended. Thus, instead of imagining

---

[3] Fox is well aware of the issues to do with literary principles and wordprocessing which he has raised and discussed in"The Fairy Queen", justWords, 2002. However, the nicest and shortest and perhaps one of the earliest useful discussions is that of Michael Rogers, "Computers and Language: An Optimistic View", in "The State of the Language", ed Christopher Ricks and Leonard Michaels, 1990, p 295-306.

2

what Deor would feel to be human, Fox imagined what it was like for an human to become a deer. The former sense would actually reduce the scope of human-being while the latter would and did extend it. The intense working up of the poem seen in the draftings below is partly caused by the problem of expressing being a deer when a deer (obviously) cannot express itself in the English language. Hence, the parallel distance set between the language of the poem and the expression of the deer (Deor).

Ultimately, of course, it is not possible to 'be' Deor, and the poem is obliged to display the inevitable compromise. It ends up only able to express the irresolvability of the paradox. The poem draws both Deor and Fox to confront the inevitability of this irresolution. It is through this confrontation that some inkling of Deor's underlying (non-verbal) being can be sensed and expressed by attending to the *desiderata*. The poem isolates what is missing in the becoming Deor. It is in this 'isolation' that the (unspoken) being Deor is specified, as it were, inside a kind of existential parenthesis. The 'readitor' is invited, even forced, to make the imaginative leap into the inevitable gap between both beings. In this way of writing Fox is attempting to evade the language trap that grips him (ineluctably) within his (English) humanity.

The title "Deor" is taken from an Old English poem of the same name, possibly originating in the 5th or 6th centuries CE in its oral form. *Deor* in Old English (which is to say Anglo-Saxon) means any creature of the wild, while *Heorot* (hart) was the Old English for deer in particular. The Old English poem is a lament, or perhaps more accurately a complaint, in which the poet took on the name *Deor* to represent his estrangement from the home and hall of his Lord. The poem expresses the poet *Deor's* sorrow and sense of loss, and can be understood as an expression of almost wholly mundane and self interested concerns. The poem is a lament for the loss of position as a court poet and, at the same time, a promotional piece advertising, or more precisely lobbying, for a new position in another, perhaps any other, court or hall. *Deor* (the *scop* - poet) was sentenced to wander outside the home and hall of his Lord, that worst of all wildernesses reserved in Old English society for the lordless. The poet (*scop*) clearly chose the name *Deor* to convey the feeling of being such an outsider, a stranger to the community of human life, as to seem a creature of the wild. Fox treats the deer Deor as a hunted being, yet a being regarded by humans as of great beauty, dignity and value. The poem "*Deor*" seems in some ways typical of that small amount of Old English lyric poetry that survives, although, it must be said that, as an Old English poem, it is of unusual form[4].

Fox's Deor turns from merely the poet with a wild animal's name, a name that intimated then the life of the deer, the *Heorot* or hart, as perceived by the Anglo-Saxon. The Old English poet's use of the name *Deor* conveys the human perception of what the life of a deer or wild animal was felt to be by the Anglo-Saxon. This is to say, as a being outside the sphere of human community and knowledge, a stranger wandering the world to no (human) purpose. The Old English poem *Deor* is thus a wholly conventional perspective on wild animals which assumes that, relative to human life, their lives cannot but be lonely and sorrowful. The purpose of their existence is to feed both the material and the imaginative needs of humankind. Fox's Deor absorbs and recognises this while introducing a shamanistic 'reality' which he winds around and threads through the conventional Old English shape of the poem. The spread of puns composed in the title "Deor *dear heart dear one*", and the reversal of the italics showing the modern English as strangely 'foreign', confirms Fox's intention.

From the draftings of "Deor *dear heart dear one*" it is clear that Fox begins to write with the broadest and roughest of brushes. His feelings about sighting and naming Deor take the form of a wordless shape or image of intense (complex) non-verbal meaning. The draftings show him trying to overcome the almost complete disconnection between his feelings, their shape, and his verbal language (English). This overcoming is shown in the draftings which gradually and carefully draw Deor from the shadows of the non-verbal gloaming inhabited by them both into the

---

[4] Apart from the standard academic references there is a useful version of the Old English text and translation at:
http://www.anglo-saxons.net/hwaet/?do=get&type=text&id=Deor

human world of words without destroying the deer. The draftings throw light on the occasional obscurity. For example,

So drink their velvet when it's shed

A slight note in the drafting gives the clue that Fox is introducing the aphrodisiac made by boiling summer antler velvet cast each year by the stags. The velvet is comprised of the sensitive hairs growing with the new antlers that emerge each year. This 'velvet' is as sensitive as cat's whiskers and acts in a similar way to tell the deer its changing width. The magical medicinal brew is said to rejuvenate the sexual powers of the human male. There are, of course, many 'natural' medicinal claims made for admixtures involving ground deer antler and summer velvet. A quick trip to the internet will provide very many sources of assurance for the needy who have in mind the magnificence of stag antlers and a natural association with sexual prowess. Apart from the stunning sightings of deer at Balmoral, and the sighting of Deor in particular, Fox was fascinated by Erwin and Peggy Baur's beautifully illustrated book[5].

"Core rite" was written at Beadnell, Northumberland in March 2007 during a stay to visit nearby Lindisfarne and Bamburgh Castle. It reflects an actual childhood memory of mine, shared with Fox, of a morning breaktime at Swaythling Primary School during the winter of 1948 when I wheedled the said apple core from a passing playmate in the school yard. In 1948 apples were everso rare, particularly in a school serving a large and decidedly unwealthy, if well ordered, and only moderately bombed council estate. The scrounging of cores was not uncommon in those days of scarcity, considerations of hygiene being of limited scope and influence in the minds of the deprived. It is almost certain that this apple was pinched and trousered by a docker at Southampton docks. A lot of dockers lived with their families on the estate. Dockers' kids were the envy of us all. It was not unknown for them to even come to school with a banana! The hidden privileges and benefits of being the child of a butter, indeed light fingered docker were

---

[5] Erwin A Baur, "Antlers: the antlered animals of Europe and North America", Swan Hill Press UK, 1995.

notorious. The action was thus to do with the six year old haves and have nots on the estate. The tiny Eve's reference to "Tear" is to Terry, known then as "ar Tair". Fox, all these years later, caught in this "Core" poem the heart of that exchange, its innocence and its complex accretion of experience.

Fox consistently eschews the clueless 'crossword' puzzle approach to poetry; as it were, the presentation out of the blue of a bunch of bare words deposited on blank paper in the naive expectation that the 'readitor' will commit huge intellectual and emotional energy to puzzling it out of its recondite repository into the open. Such 'readitors' are truly rare, and, in any case, who has got time to allot to such unnecessary effort? A few additional clues seem to Fox not a bad thing in this wildly disparate world where the familiar well trodden woods of poetry in English have become a vast and indeterminate jungle full of poems which roam and run, scurry and scrawl, wild creatures, hurrying, strange, unseen, unknown, unknowable living beings ineluctably entangled in unknown earths foxed among roots of trees so diverse as to leave the woods wholly unseen. If you see what I mean.

By the way the draftings pages are numbered by hand and encircled roughly in the order they were written. Thus, their appearance in the book pagination seems wrong ordered according to the book, but not according to the writing itself.

Thanks as always to Siriluck for her kind support and encouragement. Very much appreciated too is her skill and artistic insight in creating the beautiful cover illustration with its extraordinarily loving detail. Appreciation too for the kind help of George and Malvina Mihov of Skriptorium Ltd in bringing this work to print, and to Lizzy Attree for a final reading.

Terry Edwards, August 2007, at
Keynsham, Somerset, England.

Deor
dear heart dear one

As the narrow day was gloaming
You know the deer were surely roaming
Down the tracks 'til they trespass
Upon this luscious lower grass

There among the fir and pine
You could see their sign
And hear the way the heather moves
Beneath the touch of tender hooves

A flick a bob the slightest stone
Tells you that you're not alone
Yet it's as if they've passed you by
No matter how you strain your eye

Tired and weeping over-strained
You feel your being has been drained
For both your eyes are moist as deer
Whose fearful presence seems so near

So near those eyes confuse your sight
Whose tears involve the failing light
To form a creature out of space
From your vision of that place

Thus this shape begins to haunt
These shadows where you hunt
Here nothing seems to be quite right
No matter how you strain your sight

For in a world of make believe
Your dear heart can but conceive
Its being beaten into view
As if in blood it had come true

So it seems your world is hell
Here in the narrow pass and spell
Where sharp goblins hide among the trees
Whose sudden sight your blood must freeze

But if you miss the annual cull
Your antlers fixed upon your skull
Their branch and fork and subtle tine
Prove that you are pure cervine

Each year afresh your rack is grown
And yet again its salve is thrown
To those who know its strength to cure
All those failings men endure

So drink their velvet when it's shed
And plant those antlers in your head
Where thereof they're wholly wed
For in one being we are bled

By that blessing quick and fast
As one another firmly cast
How could you tell your blood from mine
Too fleetly running to themselves divine

For in one life it's all the same
We find ourselves to be the game
In which the others cut their stakes
While all we know is what it takes

To be a creature wild and free
The dearest thing that you can be
For your heart is turned to one
If this freedom can be won

For freedom in each other's eyes
Seems a blessing in disguise
But it's hard to be alone
Far beyond what has been known
Where you find that you are mine
Here within the fir and pine

The Drafts

Vision ①

Living with myself was hard   shard

While among the firs & pines
I could but see their signs
Imagining deer at every clump   lump
Emerging as heather moves   hump
As the wind carried   hooves   hump
   the sound of their   jump
           white rump
Muffled in fog   tramp

While among the firs & pines
Yes I could see their signs
Just as the day was glowing   curbing
At the dusk   forming
     roaming   homing

And learnt to way the heather moves
To the careful movement of those hooves
   heather tread

At the narrow day was fading
There at onenight the firs & pines
You could see their signs

14

Tired and weeping with ~~their~~ strain of
Your eyes are moist just as the deer

moist

You feel your being has been drawn
For both y' eyes are moist as deer
Who see you in their parent

Through the gloom toward the green
So they

to, bring themselves toward the grass
To find their way to quietly
~~To bring themselves~~

Upon the luscious lower grass

To take their paths to t' trespass

The tracks that wound

Down the tracks til they could trespass

A flick a bob the slightest stone
Tells Told you that you're not alone
But for eyes
yet no matter how you strain y' eyes

Surely they are all have you in sight
Let it say if they've
tell you know he's passed you by
No matter how you strain y' eyes

③

As the narrow day was glooming
You knew the deer were surely roaming
Draw their tracks ~~for they~~ trespass
+   Upon the luscious lower grass

There among the fir & pine
You could see their sign
And hear the way the heather moves
~~To the tender tread of the grooves~~
Beneath the tread of tender hooves

A flick a bob the slightest stone
Tells you that you're not alone
Yet it's as if they've passed you by
No matter how you strain your eye

Tired and weeping over-strained
You feel your being has been drained
For both your eyes are worth a deer
Whose fearful presence seems so near

So near those eyes confuse your sight
Whose tears involved with failing light
Form a creature out of space &
In your vision of that place &

16 Dear — Robert Fulls silo

Gordon — p. 79

(6) Alesander — P.36/ 43

Strophic form — 4 stanzas

dyre = dear
Deer — wild animal

vision
to Disney deer dear Bambi
deor
dyre

So near those eyes confuse your sight
Whose tears involved with failing light
Form a creature out of space
In your vision of that place

14

Bullockshui.

narrow ravine ? of hobgoblin → / foru
or place :

Harrow mountain } barracks
Pass (5)

Tired and weeping over-strained.
You feel your being has been drowned
For both your eyes are moist and dee
For here your presence is too near
heavy here
Whose fearful presence seems so near
fearful

So near you eyes seem
nestling confuse your sight
tears upon the faulting light
So near those eyes confuse you sight
White tears involved with faulting light

Superb
Create a vision of the strong   bag
Obscure   crag.
Appearing   vision.   Cag
       hug
Is a Creature of you   Iray
       say
       tog

out of space
Form a creature from the ____

In your vision of that place
As if it

15

⑧

Such blessing seems a ~~mark~~ ^sign^ divine
For who could tell your blood from mine

As if by magic quick and ^flick^ ^sharp^
~~Such~~   quick

For in the magic all was quick

Wild the animal ^haunts^ joined as one
                ~~hunt~~
                ~~haunt~~

Aphrodisiac
recipe
they had to tear

And drank their velvet when it shed
To put those antlers on my head
And so your place was wholly wed
Into one being we had bled
As in

who could tell your blood from mine
Blessing seems a mark divine
For neither could divine
A difference the creature that was made
To stand before
                    stamped

cheat? rejuvenate
weapon   Width — the poet's lament
Heart   & Deer — dying run
Hart   88 — a book
antlers   a riddle 93 -
the wisdom   ?,   (7)

without space you place it at one   war

[The weapon of your heart]

The animal wild   ———→

                    You being
Here you find the animal wild   child
                    are
As the au animal   beguiles   guiles

Heart Hart

The Aid way that creature seems to fit
Upon your own head to be it   bit fit.
For as that creature seems to fit
They were there their weight   ———→

Thus creature out of space became

Out of space creature came

                                   same
                                   bled
    hunting   bread
A haunting   fled
                                   head
And when those antlers

And drank their velvet when it shed
Ate put those antlers on my head
whist   for.
And as your place was wholey   wed
A single being we had   filed
Into one being we had bled

which only they

That rue to ones of divine
when all that ran for on

⑩ Running swiftly fleetly for th

And by that blessing quick & fast
As one another   firmly cast
Who then could could tell yr blood from mine
As if such.   divine

By that blessing quick & fast
As one another firmly cast
Who could tell your blood from mine
But only   in themselves divine
When only / in   one self
That only in / that
For in its blood
Brooding by ourself divine
Brooded in one self divine

No matter   self divine

Not with hazel or the twig own your self divine

Not with hazel nor with twig / your self divine
Not with knife nor with   dig jig.
or

Open up

Too fleetly running to themselves divine
For in our life there's not just not much chance
It's all the same
we find ourselves no more than gone

alienated from Christ Love
alienated from (his) world
alienated for — reader
auditor

⑨

And drank their velvet when it shed
To put those antlers on my head
Which to that place they wholly wend
Into one being we had bled
For in   were

                    or disguise
By that blessing quick and fast
As one another firmly cast
How could you tell your blood fractions
Too fleetly running to themselves divine

For in one life it's all the same
We first ourselves to be the game
    that we are the   to
To which the others cut for stakes
And all we know of what it takes
                              they
We find it's we that is the game
                    are

    It is as if we take the blame

                    eyes
    disguise size ties
              flies lies
              rise dies
                         pries
              cries prize
              vies wise

(2)

For in one life it's all the same
We find ourselves to be the game
Played out across this scene or that
          and beaten in a scene
Not us
Taken from the scene

Whose stakes are played out

Played out for stakes cut from real life
          chance
                    cut   for
To which the others play their stakes
Playing out the time it takes
While we know just what it takes
But   that

For in one life it's all the same
We find ourselves to be the game
In which the others cut for stakes
While we feel just what it takes
     Yet   that

A game that's played for what it takes
   And play with us

And all we know is what it takes

The dearness of my being

→ Your being to me the dearest thing

To be a that

all creatures wild & free be
The dearest thing that are can be

Beloved   agree
                                            decree
      in his
For   our shape is not me   See,
      in this   me
                                         are

                              has passed on by
Which though believed day

                                         try
                                         fly
              Sealised's   cry

         heartfelt shape flicked

(14)

Seen as one Young

In that chrysa we are made as one

dove war

brave

pain

your Sun

Cross our path

That lived the feeling

Seen For freedom in each other's eyes
as a blessing in disguise

But it's hard to be alone
Far beyond what has been known
Where you find that you are mine
Here among the fir & pine

(13)

For
Yet it's something hard to be alone
all you'd known known
Far beyond what you'd been had known
Here among the fir and pine
Where there to you find that you are mine

Because
Although
For that freedom in some eyes
and
Is a blessing in disguise

brand
bred   for freedom in
but   each other's eyes

For
Yet each freedom in some eyes
Is a blessing in disguise
When

/   hunt haunt

As if a blessing in disguise

But freedoms is a blessing

(16)

That makes believe

This dim shape begins to haunt
These shadows where we hunt
~~Haunt the~~
For nothing seems exactly right
As if a substance came to be

Though nothing seems to be quite right
No matter how the strain our sight

Exact
fact

Where nothing seems to be exact
As if   was a fact
          is

This dim shape begins to haunt
These shadows where you hunt
Here nothing seems to be quite right
No matter how you strain your sight

Substance   Hunted / haunted / hung
                   a / trophy

                                    Sophy (15)

For we can see
    there they are
For they are there

    Such in sight taken in

              taken in
    By the shadows of the shows
              of their

    Oh they shadows taken in

    By mere shadows taken in

There is nothing but the hunt
              the shape that seem to haunt

There is nothing but to hunt
For those shapes that seem to haunt

              Dear
                        a   haunt
From whose this shape is made to fit
                        put
Whose eyes forever seem to hunt   take
Which from nothing take the shape   right
                                                 — jope
              seems to haunt

Whose eyes can never stop   to hunt
              only seems

Their substance   haunt

28

⑱

Salve
Cohui
elixir
Cmeasuring potion
healing

Your dear heart is

But your dear heart ~~does not~~ cannot conceive
In a world of make believe

For a world of make believe
Your dear heart can but conceive

The shape it beats to cee grieve
in place leave
fare lose
grace cure

By
A magic in its base

For in a world of make believe

The sherry beating into ~~the~~ shape
beaten view

By

With pulsing blood   true

As if with blood you'd come quite
by   true

For it,
Yet in a world of make believe   grieve
                                           conceive

For all you dear heart

                    can conceive
          In this world of make believe

For in a world of make believe
You dear heart can but conceive
The shape it beats in place
Itself the being as   gaps

Whose shape it beats in place
      form   shape

Its being beaten into view
                                    here
As if by blood you'd come true
                    had   /

For in a world of make believe
You dear heart can but conceive
Its being beaten into view
As if by blood it had come true

Warwick
Balloch — In the narrow pass & spell
Bin — goblin

Where in the narrow pass & spell
It seem'd a world in hell
So it seem'd you world was hell
Here in the narrow pass and spell
Where goblins the in y'r blood to freeze
hide among the trees
Whose sudden sight y'r blood must freeze

So it seems your world is hell
Here in the narrow pass and spell
Where goblins force your blood to freeze
whose sudden sight blood will freeze

Where goblins hide among the trees
Whose sudden sight y'r blood must freeze

So it seems your world is hell
Here in the narrow pass and spell
Where goblins hide among the trees
Whose sudden sight y'r blood must freeze

Ruck
Pedicle   forks
Beams
Brandle
Twies

But gollen task

Thus in a moment all seems clear   dees

annual
fall till Each year   new
                                                 yene
annual
shedding In the power & prestige   cervine

All → pain and sudden end
                            send fend
All seems
              shape drape

Each year afresh year rack → grow   again
To shed its Salve   thrown
  drape   its Salve → thrown
And once again its Salve → thrown
                                  power to
To those who know its cure pure
            know   sure
                                   endure
                                   cure
upon the gaping earth

   If drunk

As elixir healing   pure
whose healing
Man's weakness
their's weakness they must endure
All those weakness men

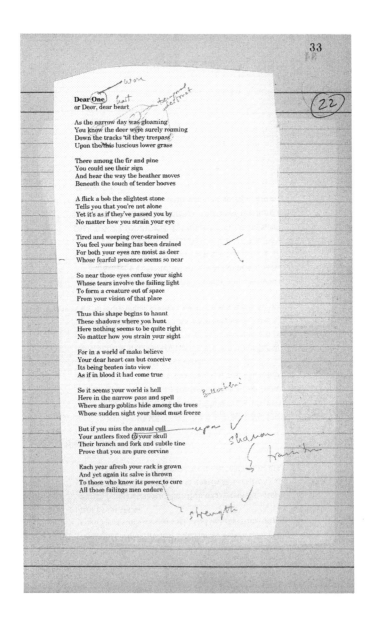

Dear One
or Deor, dear heart

As the narrow day was gloaming
You know the deer were surely roaming
Down the tracks 'til they trespass
Upon the this luscious lower grass

There among the fir and pine
You could see their sign
And hear the way the heather moves
Beneath the touch of tender hooves

A flick a bob the slightest stone
Tells you that you're not alone
Yet it's as if they've passed you by
No matter how you strain your eye

Tired and weeping over-strained
You feel your being has been drained
For both your eyes are moist as deer
Whose fearful presence seems so near

So near those eyes confuse your sight
Whose tears involve the failing light
To form a creature out of space
From your vision of that place

Thus this shape begins to haunt
These shadows where you hunt
Here nothing seems to be quite right
No matter how you strain your sight

For in a world of make believe
Your dear heart can but conceive
Its being beaten into view
As if in blood it had come true

So it seems your world is hell
Here in the narrow pass and spell
Where sharp goblins hide among the trees
Whose sudden sight your blood must freeze

But if you miss the annual cull
Your antlers fixed to your skull
Their branch and fork and subtle tine
Prove that you are pure cervine

Each year afresh your rack is grown
And yet again its salve is thrown
To those who know its power to cure
All those failings men endure

30

②

Each year after your rack is grown
And once again it's solve it thrown
To those who know its power to cure
All those weaknesses men might endure
~~madly frailties~~
~~failings~~

But if you miss the ~~animal~~ (yearly) cull
Keep yr antlers fixed to your skull
~~And the~~ branches ~~splits~~ forks & tines
between each   prove carnine

So in the end you ~~prove carnine~~
Raised to prove   [stop]
                   [plot]
Prove that you are ~~pure~~ carnine

But if you miss the animal cull
Keep your antlers fixed to your Skull
Their branch and fork & subtle tine

And
So drink their velvet when its shed
To plant those antlers in your head
Which to that place they wholly wed
For in one being we are bled

Where therein theyre wholly wed

By that blessing quick and fast
As one another firmly cast
How could you tell your blood from mine
Too fleetly running to themselves divine

For in one life it's all the same
We find ourselves to be the game
In which the others cut their stakes
While all we know is what it takes

To be a creature wild and free
The dearest thing that ~~you can only~~ can be
For your heart is turned to one
If this freedom can be won

For freedom in each other's eyes
Seems a blessing in disguise
But it's hard to be alone
Far beyond what has been known
Where you find that you are mine
Here within/~~among~~ the fir and pine

Dear One
or Deor, dear heart

As the narrow day was gloaming
You know the deer were surely roaming
Down the tracks 'til they trespass
Upon this luscious lower grass

There among the fir and pine
You could see their sign
And hear the way the heather moves
Beneath the touch of tender hooves

A flick a bob the slightest stone
Tells you that you're not alone
Yet it's as if they've passed you by
No matter how you strain your eye

Tired and weeping over-strained
You feel your being has been drained
For both your eyes are moist as deer
Whose fearful presence seems so near

So near those eyes confuse your sight
Whose tears involve the failing light
To form a creature out of space
From your vision of that place

Thus this shape begins to haunt
These shadows where you hunt
Here nothing seems to be quite right
No matter how you strain your sight

For in a world of make believe
Your dear heart can but conceive
Its being beaten into view
As if in blood it had come true

So it seems your world is hell
Here in the narrow pass and spell
Where sharp goblins hide among the trees
Whose sudden sight your blood must freeze

But if you miss the annual cull
Your antlers fixed upon your skull
Their branch and fork and subtle tine
Prove that you are pure cervine

Each year afresh your rack is grown
And yet again its salve is thrown
To those who know its strength to cure
All those failings men endure

So drink their velvet when its shed
And plant those antlers in your head
Where thereof they're wholly wed
For in one being we are bled

By that blessing quick and fast
As one another firmly cast
How could you tell your blood from mine
Too fleetly running to themselves divine

For in one life it's all the same
We find ourselves to be the game
In which the others cut their stakes
While all we know is what it takes

To be a creature wild and free
The dearest thing that you can be
For your heart is turned to one
If this freedom can be won

For freedom in each other's eyes
Seems a blessing in disguise
But it's hard to be alone
Far beyond what has been known
Where you find that you are mine
Here within the fir and pine

Core rite
(gi' us yer core mate)

gi' us yer core mate
was what I said
then in those days of it
the war being it
and the days after scarce of it
food being it by then

'e 'ad an appal didn 'e
yeh
amazin
not a care about him of 'er and all that
no
didn't give a fuck did 'e
just et it
the appal being it

juicy it was
the noise of it
the crunching being it
and the juice being juice
like it couldn't 'elp itself

me I could taste it
it being the sound of it
'is eat ing it there in the school yard
in my face
oblivious of it
my face being it

'e just knew it

it being the appal right

near the end of it
it being me waiting
I got me bid in

'gi 'us yer core mate

'e
replete of appal said
'orright mate
'e et a bit more, right
an' give it me, right
gave it me 'is core, right
an I 'ad it in me 'and

she
called me quick, see
gi 'us yer core Tear

me art stopped
fuck
she was quick, right
gettin at me core

an I give it 'er
me core, right

it didn't make sense
it being my core, an that
but she missed 'er apple too
so I gave it 'er, right
it being my core, right
the bit left of it that 'e gave me
what's 'is name's appal, right

she et it
the whole lot
swallowed it pips an all
an that was it, see

Gi us yer core mate 1

Gi us yer core mate
who
was which I said
Then — three days of it
The war being it
And the days after Scared of it
Food being it by then

He had an apple
yes
Amazing
Not a care about him
Of her and all that
No
Didn't give a fuck
Just eat it
The apple being it
Juicy it was
The noise of it
The crunching being it
And the juice being
Juice
Like it couldn't help itself

Me I could taste it
It being the sound of it
Him eating it there in the
                    School yard
In my face oblivious of it
my face being it

Core

②

~~Hette~~ He knew the apple
That was it

Hear the end of it
my writing
I got my bit in
Gi us your core mate

He
Replete of apple said
Oright mate
Gave me his core

She call me quick
Gi us the core Tom
My heart stopped
Fuck
She was quick

I gave her my core
It didn't make sense
It being my core
But she wanted her apple too
So I gave it her
It being my core
The remainder of what's it name's
Apple.

Blackwell
2007